KIA A. DURHAM

AS FOR ME AND MY HOUSE

A 21-DAY PRAYER JOURNEY

ELOHAI
INTERNATIONAL
PUBLISHING & MEDIA

Praise for *As For Me and My House*

"This book will help you and your family unpack the gifts God has for you that are wrapped and packaged with your prayer life. The author of this book is a spiritual general in the 82nd Prayer Division of the Army of The Lord and this book is basic training. I pray that it blesses you and your family the way it has impacted me. It balances being both practical and spiritual, motivational, and relatable. Use this time to reconnect with your family, to teach your children why Jesus said that, 'Man should always pray and not faint.' This book makes teaching that principle to future generations easy. You will be blessed when you declare that 'As for me and my house we will serve the Lord,' and this book will help guide your prayer life as the Holy Spirit makes that statement true."

—Rev. Daniel C. Bradley, The Genius Group

"*As For Me and My House* is a spiritually charged resource that will equip families with the most powerful and transformative tool—prayer, that by God's Grace will allow them to reach new realms of spiritual growth as a family. I believe that by the end of the twenty-one day journey, many families will make the decision to serve God wholeheartedly, being able to quote the very same words that Minister Kia and her family stand on from the book of Joshua, 'As for me and my house, we will serve the Lord' (Joshua 24:15)."

—April Fields, Women of Grace, Faith & Courage

"Min. Kia Durham's inspirational guide for families to walk together in faith could not be more fitting for today. All families feel the chaos of the world and *As For Me and My House* offers a timeless, calming solution. Min. Durham's devotion to her Christian foundation is beautifully embodied and allows her to provide families spiritual growth guidance applicable to all faiths."

—Michelle Azu, MD

"As a woman of prayer, I know first-hand how important it is to pray. Prayer gets us through our difficult times in life. Prayer gives us guidance. Prayer is our lifeline to God. This book will benefit children, parents, and all who know the power of prayer. Thank you Minster Kia for walking in the call of God for your life."

—Linda Lee, DC Department of Employment Services

"I was so moved by the premise and focus of this book. Most prayer books focus on the individual, but this book emphasizes the family, which will have a direct and measurable generational impact. For the parents, we will learn to obey God's commandment to train up the child towards Him; and for the children, they will learn that seeking God should be as important as breathing. Thanks, Minister Kia, for your obedience and commitment to the kingdom. It is needed."

—Antwanye Ford, Enlightened, Inc.

"*As For Me And My House* is an essential book that EVERY home should have. And a book that every home should come with, right alongside their new home welcome packet. It is the perfect book that provides much needed insight, instructions, and inspiration for every family, collectively and individually about praying together. The push for family prayer allows for encouragement and conviction to pour off the pages. Kia challenges her readers to get back to the basics of family bonding, through family praying. We all know how much prayer is needed in the world, but it starts at home As I was reading, I immediately began to search my own prayer life to see how I can incorporate even more prayer for me and my family! My family will be better because of this book, and I know your family will be better also."

—Danny Prince II, Husband, Father, Teen Pastor,
Author, and Youth & Teen Advocate

As for Me and My House: A 21-Day Prayer Journey

Copyright © 2021 by Kia A. Durham

Published by ELOHAI International Publishing & Media
P.O. Box 1883
Cypress, TX 77410

Website: www.elohaipublishing.com
Email: hello@elohaiintl.com

Scripture quotations taken from the (NASB®) New American Standard Bible®, Copyright © 2020 by The Lockman Foundation. Used by permission. All rights reserved. www.lockman.org.

Scriptures marked NIV are taken from the NEW INTERNATIONAL VERSION (NIV): Scripture taken from THE HOLY BIBLE, NEW INTERNATIONAL VERSION®. Copyright © 1973, 1978, 1984, 2011 by Biblica, Inc.® Used by permission of Zondervan.

Scriptures marked KJV are taken from the KING JAMES VERSION (KJV): KING JAMES VERSION, public domain.

Scriptures marked NKJV are taken from the NEW KING JAMES VERSION (NKJV): Scripture taken from the NEW KING JAMES VERSION®. Copyright © 1982 by Thomas Nelson, Inc. Used by permission. All rights reserved.

ISBN: 978-1-953535-41-2

Printed in the United States of America

Dedication

I dedicate this book to my children, Nia and AJ, for truly being a blessing in our lives and for helping mommy record our family prayers each night. I love you both to the moon and back.

I dedicate this book to my mom, Joyce, for being super supportive and for assisting us with the actual recordings. You are the best, mom!!

Last, but certainly not least, I dedicate this book to Anthony, my loving husband, for your never-ending love, encouragement, and support throughout this process. I am so thankful and blessed by God to be your wife.

Dedication

Table of Contents

Foreword

Bishop Phillip O. Thomas
Highview Christian Fellowship, Fairfax, Virginia

It's been said that a family that prays together stays together. This is a popular phrase often heard in discussions regarding a family crisis. Yet many of us who use this expression fail to lead family lives reflective of this non-scriptural, but excellent suggestion with a strong biblical principle attached, as often as we should. We are instructed by the Apostle Paul to pray without ceasing, and Jesus gives us a present imperative with continuous action to keep asking, seeking, and knocking. In our increasingly crisis-oriented world, the author Min. Kia Durham shows parents and family members how to lead and promote godly and healthy lives through the practice and implementation of daily devotional time in prayer together in very creative ways.

Min. Durham's first book offers us a strategic and interactive approach to developing and maintaining a family lifestyle of communication with God daily. This book is destined to be added to the list of works that will continue to equip the Christian family with relevant tools to pass on a living Christian faith so that our children are prepared to follow Jesus Christ into their own adult lives.

While the pressures and morals of our society seem overwhelming, God has inspired this author to share wonderful concepts and ideas through family prayer that will be transformative indeed. Being able to redeem the time will have fresh meaning as you read and interact with this book. It will be a wonderful pathway to once again recapture family time so desperately needed and so unfortunately abandoned. As the author reminds us; as we call on God according to Jer. 33:3,

He will answer and will tell us great and hidden things that we have not known. Things like keeping our families spiritually focused and committed to the kingdom agenda from the youngest to the oldest. And how to experience victory and the joy of knowing and serving our Savior and Lord every day. Let's enjoy this first journey together! Thank God for this wonderful deposit in the earth.

Introduction to Family Prayer and Purpose for the Book

They say the family that prays together stays together. And although this phrase is not scripture, I believe it contains a lot of Godly truth and wisdom. So as a family, let's pray! Praise God you made it. As we embark on this twenty-one day journey together, let's trust God for a mighty move of the Holy Spirit within ourselves and our families.

The more I continue to grow in Christ and the closer I get to know my Father in heaven, the more I have come to realize just how much I need daily quiet times of prayer. It's during these quiet times of prayer that the Lord really speaks to my heart. It's when He fills me with the confidence I need to complete my daily tasks. It's when He rebukes me for any wrongdoing I may have done and then assures me that He still loves me and shows me the path to take and make things right. And it's also when He gives me wisdom and instruction for completing the tasks He is calling me to do. The Holy Spirit fills me with His words and leads me in the way He would have me to go—I just have to listen and obey! Truly, as the verse says, "Call to Me and I will answer you, and will tell you great and hidden things that you have not known." (Jeremiah 33:3). I call on God in prayer and *has He ever* responded and revealed His purpose and will for me!

I was having one of my quiet times reading the Lord's Word and praying when BAM. Lightbulb. It hit me. As I sat in front of my Savior, He made clear to me that He was calling me into something higher. He was calling me into not only a life dedicated to prayer, but of leading prayer and helping others to pray in His name. As I began to seek His meaning for this and what it might look like, I spent more time on my knees in His presence and journaling my journey. He began to open my eyes with illumination only the Holy Spirit can provide from within. I slowly began to watch the unbelievable become real and incredibly believable. I began to see the unattainable become the so attainable. It wasn't just in my grasp, it was greeting me everywhere I went. I began to observe the incredible become an integral part of precious daily life—simple, yet poignant and all together lovely. This was all due to intentional prayer rooted in scripture and lead by the Holy Spirit. I can't say it enough, God tells us, "Call to Me and I will answer you, and will tell you great and hidden things that you have not known" (Jeremiah 33:3). I call on God in prayer and He always reveals His purpose and will for me!

The Word of God in Joshua 24:15 says, "But as for me and my household, we will serve the LORD."

When we were blessed with children, my husband and I made the decision to have our children pray, be involved in and take part of leading family prayers, even when they were young. It was during one of these family praying times that the Holy Spirit spoke into my heart and told me to record our family prayers. This simple act of obedience was the foundation of the book you are holding in your hands right now! The Lord specifically commanded that I write this book in conjunction with my two children. My children, albeit excited and nervous, accepted the task with me... and here we are today! It's been said that out of the mouths of babes and infants, you have established strength (Psalm 8:2a ESV) and I pray that you are blessed by our family's obedience (Psalm 19:14).

Instructions Before You Begin

The following steps should help you as you and your loved ones prepare to begin this journey. Please note, as life is complicated and varied, these prayers can be prayed using different and substituted pronouns. If you are single or your spouse is unable to pray with you, use singular pronouns. If you are a couple and/or family, use plural pronouns. The prayers are written for me and my household, but all can be modified to fit your certain circumstance. The Lord will honor it! And you, singular or plural, will be blessed for it!

I.   Maintain a dedicated time and space to spend as a family with God each day. This allows for balance in the business of life. "As for me and my house, we will serve the Lord!" (Joshua 24:15b).

II. Use this time to connect as a family—discuss the highs and lows of the day. "Rejoice with those who rejoice; weep with those that weep" (Romans 12:15).

III. Be real and transparent and let the kids hear your concerns when you come to your Heavenly Father. When they hear you pray in such an authentic way—it not only shows them how to pray; it shows them how to trust God, and it shows them how to go to the Lord in prayer, according to Matthew 6:9-13 and Luke 11:2-4.

IV. Pray your respective prayers (child, parent) using this guide each day in your dedicated time and space. Remember this is the time to start praying together as a family.

V.   Use the blank spaces to write out your prayer requests, praises, and affirmations.

As you embark on this journey, remember that you are not alone. Your Heavenly Father sees you, and He believes in you. You can do this. Praying together as a family may seem like a daunting task at first, but trust God. Trust that the same God who blessed you with your children is in fact the SAME God who will bless you in this season of life, and in all seasons.

Let us pray:

Father God, we look to the hills, from where our help comes from. And Lord we know that our help comes from you (Psalm 121). And we thank You. As we embark on the next twenty-one days of prayer as a family, please bless our family. Touch each and every heart, mind, and body. In the name of Jesus, we thank You. Almighty God, for this day. Amen.

"Be anxious for nothing, but in everything by prayer and supplication with thanksgiving let your requests be made known to God." (Philippians 4:6 NASB)

Parents' Prayer Journal

Week #1, Day 1
Title: Let the Journey Begin!
Scripture: Psalm 19:14 (NIV)

*May these words of my mouth and this meditation of my heart
be pleasing in your sight, LORD, my Rock and my Redeemer.*

Parents' Prayer:

Father, as we usher in these next twenty-one days of prayer and
devotion, we ask You to change some things in our atmosphere.
We ask You to come in, shake the family up; shatter any strongholds of divisiveness; make the familiar like new; and show us
Your strength. You are our rock and deliverer! Father, we pray
that each of us will feel Your presence. We are asking for an
outpouring of Your Holy Spirit right here in the family, right
here in the house. You are our foundation, firm and strong. Let
us build upon You! We pray that we will get to know You more
deeply and have eyes to see only that which You could reveal to
us. We also ask Father, that all who come in contact with our
home and with our family would be blessed, simply because
You have blessed us so tremendously. Let them see the light
of Your love in our hearts and actions that they might want to
draw close to You. We are after Your heart, Lord. May You keep
us steadfast in our desire to serve You.

Father, we ask You to move and have Your way over everything in our lives. Heal what needs to be healed. Mend what
needs to be mended. Deliver our family members that need to
be delivered. Set us free, Father, loosen the earthly binds that
have us bound—all to Your glory, all to Your service.

We are asking for all these things in Your precious and holy
name. We ask that You just be with us now and forevermore. In
Jesus' name, we pray, amen.

_____

_____

_____

_____

_____

_____

_____

_____

_____

_____

_____

_____

_____

_____

Week #1, Day 2
Title: Open Our Eyes!
Scripture: Hosea 4:6 (KJV)

My people are destroyed for lack of knowledge.

Parents' Prayer:

Father, we thank You for another night to come together as a family. As we move forward on this twenty-one-day prayer journey, we pray that You will give us peace of mind, the kind of peace that passes all understanding. And please settle our spirits—so that when we come to You, Father, our focus is set on You, Lord and no other thing. Nothing comes before You Lord. You are our Redeemer, Father, and Friend.

We thank You for bringing us through another day. We thank You, Father, because You didn't have to do it. But we know You have gone before us to prepare things for us to do. You have paved the way and will guard us with Your angels. We thank you for getting us through another school day safely, another work day safely. Father, we thank You for our health and our strength.

Lord, we ask You to open our eyes and our ears and our minds Father, that we may hear You and see You and know You—that we can continue to share You with Your people Father. Your people are hurting Father God because they don't know the Word. Grant us knowledge and wisdom only You can give; equip us with the knowledge and tools to go out and make fishers of men, as you commanded us to. Let us share Your Word with the people Father, let them desire to draw nearer to You.

Father, we ask You to put a light in us, so that anyone who sees us will know that we are Your children. Children of the most high Father, the King of kings, Lord of lords, and Host of hosts. You are our hiding place. You know those things that we don't want to talk about, those things we don't want anybody else to know about. You are our ultimate hiding place, and we rest in You, Father.

Father, please forgive us of our sins, forgive us of anything that we've done. We bow down to You tonight; we are at Your feet, Lord, begging Your heavenly pardon for anything we've done that's not pleasing to Your sight. Please forgive us for those things today. And we praise You, Lord, for Your steadfast love—that it never ceases, that Your mercies never come to an end and are new each and every morning. Great is Your faithfulness! (Lamentations 3:22-23)

We rest in Your Grace and Your mercy; we rest in Your sovereignty; we rest in Your wonderfulness and Your awesomeness, Father. And we continue to stretch out our hands to You, in praise, worship, and adoration. Father, we magnify Your name. You alone are worthy of being praised, and we bless Your name today. In the wonderful name of Jesus, we pray, amen.

Week #1, Day 3
Title: We Are Forgiven!
Scripture: James 5:15 (NIV)

And the Prayer offered in faith will make the sick person well; the Lord will raise them up. If they have sinned, they will be forgiven.

Parents' Prayer:

Dear God, we thank You for getting us through another day safely, securely, and soundly, in Jesus' name! Some didn't wake up this morning, maybe even some of our very own family members, but we thank You, Lord, on this day because that's not our story. We thank You because on this day; that's not our journey. Father God, we thank You for getting us through.

We thank You for healing, breakthrough, and restoration. We thank You for healing our bodies, our spirits, and our souls. We thank You for healing our physical infirmities as well as our mental and spiritual. We thank You for healing all the broken and mending all that needs mending. Father God, You alone bind up the broken-hearted and heal our iniquities. We thank You in advance for the breaking of any strongholds plaguing our family.

Lord, we thank You in advance for a great day tomorrow. We thank You in advance for a great day of school, work, play, or rest—whatever tomorrow holds for us, we praise Your name in advance that it will provide us with one more time, one more opportunity, Father God, to edify and build each other up and thus glorify Your name, Father God.

Father God, we ask that You continue to bless us and empower us to be a Godly family—for Your grace is sufficient Lord, to bring us through each day! We pray that we are light in this dark world, Holy Father, that we would shine Your love to a world that is so bereft of it. We ask that You continue to keep us, and hold us, and continue to go before us. We pray that we are pleasing in Your sight. And we beg Your forgiveness, Lord, for Your mercy on anything we've done not pleasing in Your sight, Father God. In the name of Jesus, we pray. Amen.

_____

_____

_____

_____

_____

_____

_____

_____

_____

_____

_____

_____

Week #1, Day 4
Title: If He Did It Before, He Can Do It Again
Scripture: Ecclesiastes 1:9 (NIV)

What has been will be again, what has been done will be done again; there is nothing new under the sun.

Parents' Prayer:

Dear Lord, we thank You on this day for being God. We thank You that You're the God of sovereignty. We thank You that You are the God of Abraham, Isaac, and Jacob. We thank You, Father God, that You are the God of yesterday, today, and forevermore. Father God, Ecclesiastes 1:9 says there's nothing new under the sun—and we thank You, Lord, that for everything You've done before, You can do it again.

Father God, we bind, in the name of Jesus, any trace of wickedness trying to come against ourselves or our family; anything trying to come against our love before God. We submit to You, Lord, and the devil must flee. We bind the spirits of oppression, depression, fear, and anxiety, and we bind the spirit of insecurity, Father God, in the name of Jesus. You are our firm foundation, Father God. We go to You for safety, and we remain under Your protection! You are our defender and protector! We praise You Lord, for You are our banner—the One that goes before us into the battle and wins!

Father God, our fight is not against the powers and rulers of this world, but against the spiritual forces of evil. Your Word says that the weapons of this warfare are not carnal, but they are strong in You to the moving and pulling down of the strongholds. Father God, we ask that You put any strongholds under our feet. And that we're able to put on the armor You give us to protect us and use the weapons that You gave us to fight the enemy as he comes in and he tries to attack our family, our friends, our loved ones, our jobs, our finances, and anything else, Father God.

We're praying, Father God, that we mount up like an army, and that we fight strong. It is in Your name and Your name alone that we can take the devil and all that he tries to throw our way. It is in You that we can tread on the serpent! Father God, we know that we serve a God who can do exceedingly above all that we could even possibly hope and ever ask. So, we ask in Your mighty and wonderful name, Father God, that You continue to touch our heads down to the soles of our feet. Almighty God, keep us close to You, keep us safe, and keep us holy in Your name. In the wonderful name of Jesus, we pray. Amen.

_____

_____

_____

_____

_____

_____

_____

_____

_____

Week #1, Day 5
Title: This Is the Day That the Lord Has Made
Scripture: Psalm 118:24 (NASB)

This is the day which the Lord has made; Let us rejoice and be glad in it.

Parents' Prayer:

Dear God, we thank You, Lord, for bringing us through another day. We thank You for safely bringing us through and for keeping us from any hurt, harm, or danger that might come our way. On this day, we ask You for peace of mind, a gentle heart, and a renewing of our spirit and mind, Lord, that we would know what your will is and do it. In Jesus' name.

Lord, there may be one of us who had a bad day today, but God, we declare that this is the day that You have made, and we must rejoice and be glad in it. Lord, we accept there may be days that are less pleasant than others. There may be some things that we don't like. There will be ups and downs, highs and lows in life. We know there is a time for every season, a time for every activity under heaven. We thank You for the laughs, and we thank You for our cries—because ultimately, we know that You are causing all things to work together for our good because we love You. So, we stand firm in Your Word, and we claim there will be no more *bad* days in the name of Jesus!

We thank You, Lord, for Your grace and mercy. We thank You for Your sovereignty, and we thank You because You are better to us than we are to ourselves. So, in the name of Jesus, we pray in faith that You will take away all burdens, worries, sorrows, and anything else causing us to walk in despair on this day.

Thank You, God, in advance for hearing our cries and answering our prayers. We thank you that we have a Father in heaven that loves us and intercedes for us on our behalf. You know what we need even before we pray it. Thank you, Lord. Father God, we pray that we all wake up tomorrow feeling refreshed, renewed, and in good spirits. We love You, Lord, and we know that You love us. In the matchless name of Jesus, we pray, amen!

_____

_____

_____

_____

_____

_____

_____

_____

_____

_____

Week #1, Day 6
Title: Give Us a Steadfast Spirit
Scripture: Psalm 51:10 (NASB)

Create in me a clean heart, O God, And renew a steadfast spirit within me.

Parents' Prayer:

Dear God, we thank You for this day. We love You, Lord, from the top of our heads to the soles of our feet. We bless and praise Your holy name, for You are mighty and worthy of praise! We thank You for all the blessings and new things You have done for us today. Lord, we ask You to continue to bless our whole family. Give us this day our daily bread Lord. Bless each and every one of us, and be ever present in each circumstance and situation.

Lord, please draw those that don't know You closer to You on this day. Let this be the day that their hearts and minds are opened to Your saving grace and mercy. Please heal, save, and deliver our unsaved loved ones from the clutches of evil and anything that would ensnare them. And for our loved ones who do know You, Lord, we thank and praise You for that relationship, and we also pray for the continual strengthening of their faith. We pray that they continue to walk in faith; we pray they will not get weary in well-doing (2 Thessalonians 3:13). Father God, the time has come for Christians to stand up and to stop walking in fear. We need to have strong faith, in Jesus' name. You did *not* give us a spirit of timidity Lord, but a spirit of power! Of love! And self-discipline! (2 Timothy 1:7)

Father God, we ask You to forgive us of our sins—any word, thought, or deed—anything that is unlike You and unworthy of Your praise, please forgive us of those things today. Father

God we ask that You continue to keep us and clean us up, Lord. Purify our hearts. Create in us new hearts and let us be transformed by the renewing of our minds (Romans 12:2). As we take off the old clothes, please give us new ones. We need the new coat, in that we might be new people walking in You (Ephesians 4:22). The old things are behind us and we're pressing forward, looking to what is to come (Philippians 3:13). We rest in You and in the knowledge that as You dress the lilies of the field, how much more will you dress us (Matthew 6:28-29). We are anxious for nothing.

We thank You. We magnify You. We ask that You keep us covered in Your grace, mercy, and peace, Lord. In the precious name of Jesus, we pray. Amen.

_____

_____

_____

_____

_____

_____

_____

_____

_____

Week #1, Day 7
Title: We Walk in the Fruit of the Spirit
Scripture: Galatians 5:22–23 (NASB)

But the fruit of the Spirit is love, joy, peace, patience, kindness, goodness, faithfulness, gentleness, self-control; against such things there is no law.

Parents' Prayer:

Dear God, thank You for this day and for this past week. We thank you for the time we have had, and will continue to have, to come before You as a family. Father God, we thank You for safely bringing us through without any hurt, harm, or danger, Lord. We thank You for continuing to bless us, Father God. There's a family today, right now, that can't say that. We thank You, though, that You didn't find it robbery to get each and every one of us home safe, that we might be able to come and worship and fellowship together as a family one more time.

Father God, we ask that You be with all of us, that You will continue to cover our family. If there are any divisions, agendas, or anything trying to come against our family, we ask that You straighten out what's crooked, make right what's wrong, and bring us together in love like never before.

There's a way of decency and order (1 Corinthians 14:40) and Father God, we believe this applies to the family structure as well. So in the name of Jesus, we pray that all things be done with the decency and order You commanded us to maintain in Your word. If it's done in the darkness, we pray it comes to the light. If something offended a family member, we pray pure and soft hearts to handle the situation with humility and love (Galatians 5:22).

Father God, we worship and honor You on this day. We magnify Your Holy name, Father God. We are praying, resting in, and asking for a mighty moving of the Holy Spirit to save our loved ones who are not saved, to bring them closer to You, Father God. In the name of Jesus, we pray. Amen.

_____

_____

_____

_____

_____

_____

_____

_____

_____

_____

_____

_____

Week #2, Day 8
Title: We Present It All to the Father
Scripture: Philippians 4:6 (NASB)

Be anxious for nothing, but in everything by prayer and supplication with thanksgiving let your requests be made known to God.

Parents' Prayer:

Dear God, we thank You for another day. We thank You for all that You continue to do for us. Father God, as we begin week two of our prayer journey, we thank You for bringing us through thus far. We thank You for giving us the vigor to go on. We thank You for giving us the endurance to finish this prayer journey strong in You. Open our hearts, Father. Clear our minds of distraction. Keep us focused on You. That we will continue to walk in Your way, according to Your Word.

We thank You Lord, in advance for Your provisions, and we know that You will prepare a table for us in the presence of our enemies and that our cup will runneth over (Psalm 23:5). Father God, please bless our entire family—the children, spouses, and significant others, as well as our parents, friends, church members, co-workers, neighbors, etc. Touch each and every person, as well as each and every situation and circumstance.

We thank You in advance for the answered prayers we will receive during this time, in Jesus' name, for we know that if we seek, we shall find (Matthew 7:7). We thank You for making a way out of no way for in You, all things are possible. Father God, we know that when things don't look the way we want them to look, when it doesn't seem like things are working together for us, Father God, that's exactly when You are working all things out for our good. And we thank You for that Father today.

In this world today, the Christian walk is not always easy and it requires confidence and faith in You. So, we're praying for confidence to the insecure, faith to the faithless, hope to the hopeless, and salvation to the unsaved.

We can't thank You and praise Your name enough. We are so thankful for Your divine providence and the loving kindness You show us each and every day. Please put a hedge of protection around us, Father God, and keep us safe from any harm and danger. In Your precious and holy name, we pray, amen!

_____

_____

_____

_____

_____

_____

_____

_____

_____

_____

Week #2, Day 9
Title: Bless the Children
Scripture: Psalm 8:2a (NASB)

From the mouth of infants and nursing babes You have established strength.

Parents' Prayer:

Father God, we thank You for being God. We thank You for bringing us through another day safely Lord God, and bringing us together again tonight. Thank You for being better to us than we are to ourselves. Thank You for Calvary and what You did on the cross. Thank You for Your grace, Your mercy, and Your sovereignty.

Lord God, thank You that You are El Shaddai (Genesis 17:1-2)—the God who is more than enough, and we thank You, God, for blessing us with more than enough. Thank You in advance for blessing us with not only our needs but also with the desires of our hearts (Psalm 37:4).

Father God, we are on this prayer journey together, a family united in You. We are Your faithful servants, being obedient in our daily prayer time, bringing our petitions and supplications before You, in humble gratitude (Philippians 4:6). We ask You to continue guiding us and leading us into the way You would have us to go. Please give us the knowledge and understanding to be able to adequately study Your word in order to share the gospel with Your people. The Bible says that Your people perish because they don't know the truth, Lord God, so please reveal Your truth to us that we may be able to share it with all those we encounter. We need more of You Jesus, the world needs more of You. It's a cold, dishonest, and deceitful world—but with You, we can, in Jesus, be victorious in all things.

Father God, make us the light in the darkness. Light will always overcome darkness. Darkness cannot overcome light. So please make us a light in the dark world. Bless the children as they grow. We pray for our boys and girls that they will grow up to be strong young men and women who love the Lord and their families. Give our children the necessary fortitude required to do well in school. Bless them to receive and master their classwork effectively. We pray they grow into men and women after your own heart, the next generation of workers in the Kingdom of God. We pray they are well, healthy, and joyous. Please give us what we need to be able to give them what they need. In Jesus' name we pray, amen.

_____

_____

_____

_____

_____

_____

_____

_____

_____

_____

Week #2, Day 10
Title: We Find Strength in Christ Jesus
Scripture: Psalm 46:1 (KJV)

God is our refuge and strength, A very present help in trouble.

Parents' Prayer:

Thank You, Lord, for this day. We thank you for bringing us through the highways and byways of life safely. We thank You for waking us up this morning and seeing that no weapons formed against us have prospered (Isaiah 54:17).

We ask that You put a hedge of protection around us to keep us safe. Send down Your angels to guide and watch over us and to protect us from the harm of this world seen and the world unseen. We know You have a plan for our lives (Jeremiah 29:11), so please God, let Your angels surround us that we might have peace, allowing us to focus on You and Your will for our lives. We stand against anything that is not of You Lord. Anything that has found its way into our lives that is not of You, we pray that it be removed, in the name of Jesus.

We pray for wisdom, knowledge, and understanding as we bring up our children in the way they should go, that they may not depart from it when they have grown (Proverbs 22:6). As the children go through the day, give them wisdom, knowledge, and understanding appropriate for them. Give them the discernment to do those things that are right. Bless each and every teacher, faculty member, school support staff, and school administrator in the name of Jesus. They each hold such an important position in the lives of the children so we cover them all in prayer today, Father God. May the knowledge they impart to our children be in line with Your word, Lord.

We pray that each and every person that comes into the lives of our children throughout the day will have a good heart and gentle spirit. We pray that no one with an ill-will, bad intentions, or anyone seeking to do harm would be allowed even remotely near our children. We entrust them into Your care, Father God, for just as You are our Abba Father, You are theirs.

We can't predict one day to the next and we definitely can't even pretend to know all the secrets of life. But You are the One we can count on as being constant. You are the one source we can depend on. You are our comfort and our present help in our time of need (Psalm 46:1–3). We know that You will always be there for us, regardless of what is going on. Your love never fails! And there is nothing in this world that can separate us from it, and we thank you for that. In the name of Jesus, we pray amen!

_____

_____

_____

_____

_____

_____

_____

_____

_____

Week #2, Day 11
Title: Today We Walk in Forgiveness
Scripture: 2 Corinthians 1:4 (NASB)

who comforts us in all our affliction so that we will be able to comfort those who are in any affliction with the comfort with which we ourselves are comforted by God.

Parents' Prayer:

Father God, thank You so much for bringing us through another day. In this day and age, some families have witnessed some of the worst things humanity has to offer, and they suffer because of it. We pray they receive Your love. We pray they receive Your peace, rest, and joy, in Jesus' name. We pray for the families who have suffered from mass shootings, gun violence, domestic abuse, incest, disease, mental illness, and things too deeply painful and terrible to speak, but God You know. We pray healing for them today.

You are the God of more than enough, and we thank You for provisions, food on our table, a roof over our heads, and all the other things we need. We thank You, Jesus, for our health and our strength.

Please, God, forgive us of our sins, and for anything that we have done, that is not pleasing in Your sight. We pray that You take those old things away and that You make our hearts new. Lord God we thank You in advance for Your most gracious forgiveness and mercies, for those are new every morning!

Father God, as You called us to forgive as You forgave us, we also pray for a spirit of forgiveness. As we are dealing with family, friends, co-workers, neighbors, even those who mean to cause us harm—please help us to forgive them. Please continue to assist us in our walk in forgiveness today and every day.

If we are going to become more like You, Father God, we have to forgive like You, in the name of Jesus and in the power of the Holy Spirit. We claim that over ourselves and over our families today—forgiveness! We are your faithful servants, and we ask that You please receive our prayers today. In the precious name of Jesus, we pray! Amen!

_____

_____

_____

_____

_____

_____

_____

_____

_____

_____

_____

Week #2, Day 12
Title: We Choose the Lord
Scripture: Joshua 25:14a (NASB)

If it is disagreeable in your sight to serve the Lord, choose for yourselves today whom you will serve...

Parents' Prayer:

Father God, we thank You for this day and for another opportunity to see Your greatness, Your wonders, and Your glory. We thank You for providing clothes on our backs, shoes on our feet, food on our table, and shelter over our heads. We thank You for our family and friends. We thank You for the good times we had today. We even thank You for the not-so-good times because we know that You are causing all things to work together for our good because we love You (Romans 8:28). We know that our light and momentary troubles are achieving for us an eternal glory that far outweighs them all! (2 Corinthians 4:17)

We pray our children will continue to have opportunities and experiences that will build them up mentally, physically, and spiritually. We pray that they will be healthy, whole, complete, smart, educated, and that they have all they need to be first and foremost believers and secondly, able to compete in this world. Bless their hearts, bless their minds, create in them a new heart. Please, God, direct their mindset and focus to You.

We pray they love You and that they receive You for themselves. We can only give them what we have but ultimately the decision is theirs to make. Your word says that we must all choose whom we will serve (Joshua 24:15). We pray in faith that when the time has come for them to make their choice, they will choose You for themselves and follow You. We pray they receive the message of the cross for themselves, on the inside. We pray that they learn to turn over all of their problems and hardships to You Father God. We pray all these things in faith. In the name of Jesus, we pray, amen!

_____

_____

_____

_____

_____

_____

_____

_____

_____

_____

_____

_____

_____

Week #2, Day 13
Title: We Choose Righteousness
Scripture: James 4:17 (NASB)

Therefore, to one who knows the right thing to do and does not do it, to him it is sin.

Parents' Prayer:

Father God, we thank You so much for this day and for bringing us through safely and securely. We thank You for this time to come together in fellowship and prayer as a family and to lift-up one another.

Please forgive us of our sins today Father God. If anyone within our family has done anything that's unbecoming in Your sight, we ask that You forgive us today of those things. Sins of omission or commission—in Your eyes are one and the same… so whatever it is today, we thank You in advance for forgiveness.

Bless the children as they go to school, make friends, and do their classwork. Please help the children discern what is right and what is pure. Assist them in their decision-making, and lead and guide them into all truth (John 16:13). Please continue to bless them and keep them safe. Keep them at the foot of the cross, and don't let them turn their backs on it.

Father God, help our family to always speak the truth, in kindness and with love. Teach us how to trust You Father God, and how to trust Your Word for our lives. Lord, Your Word says that when the enemy comes in like a flood, Your Spirit will lift up a standard against him (Isaiah 59:19). So we thank you, God, for raising up that standard against the enemy every time he tries to come against our lives and our homes or our families. In fact, we thank you for all the promises in Your Word, Lord God, and the fact that we can stand on those promises, Lord God, because Your Word also says that the answers to Your promises are yes and amen (2 Corinthians 1:20).

Lord God, we worship You and magnify Your name. God bless Your holy name! We ask that You show us the way that we should go, please give us Your Wisdom and understanding. Send Your Holy Spirit down, and please give us comfort and counsel, Father God, in our times of struggle. In the name of Jesus we pray, amen!

_____

_____

_____

_____

_____

_____

_____

_____

_____

_____

_____

Week #2, Day 14
Title: Keep Us in Your Perfect Peace
Scripture: 1 Peter 5:7 (NASB)

…casting all your anxiety on Him, because He cares for you.

Parents' Prayer:

Father God, thank You for this time. Thank You for allowing us to see another day. We thank You for Your provisions. We thank You for the food, clothing, and shelter that You have provided for us. We thank You Father God, because our needs could be much greater, but they aren't. We thank You for that today Father God. We thank You today and every day for being Jehovah-Jireh, our Provider (Genesis 22:14).

We thank You for all that You've done for us. We thank You because You are better to us than we are to ourselves. We thank You today… even when it seems like things are down and out. Even when it seems like everyone is against us or that our backs are against the wall, we can rest in knowing that You have us. We can rest knowing that You love us and that You care for us. We cast our cares on You, Father God, because You care for us (1 Peter 5:7) and we thank You Jesus! We thank You for all You did for us at the cross!

Please heal our spirits, soul, and bodies today, Father God. Touch and bless anything that has fallen out of alignment with Your perfect will. You keep in perfect peace those who trust in You, and in You we trust and believe (Isaiah 26:3). By Your stripes, we are healed! In the name of Jesus, we pray that we get through the night and next day safely. We thank You in advance for waking us up tomorrow with a renewed vigor for life.

Thank You for the gift of Your Holy Spirit. Thank You for the comfort and the counsel that He always gives us. Thank You that we can depend on the Holy Spirit to never let us down. No matter what's going on, we know that we have a Comforter that is always with us and interceding on our behalf (Romans 8:26). We pray that You continue to rest, rule, and abide in us now forth and forevermore. In the name of Jesus we pray, amen!

_____

_____

_____

_____

_____

_____

_____

_____

_____

_____

Week #3 Day 15
Title: We Claim Healing
Scripture: Isaiah 54:17 (NKJV)

No weapon formed against you shall prosper, And every tongue which rises against you in judgment You shall condemn. This is the heritage of the servants of the Lord, And their righteousness is from Me," Says the Lord.

Parents' Prayer:

Father God, we thank You for this time, we thank You for this day. We thank You for getting us to and from our destinations safely this day Father God. We thank You for Your grace and mercy, we thank You that no weapon formed against us was allowed to prosper (Isaiah 54:17), and will never prosper! We thank You for the community You have blessed us with, our work community, our church community, our neighborhood community. We thank You in advance for all of the positive influences we have to help us and keep us on the right path.

In a world full of darkness, we thank You for the miracles You show us each and every day. We thank You for all of our answered prayers. We even thank You for unanswered prayers, Lord, for You are the all-knowing God and You know what we need. We thank You for the moving of the Holy Spirit over so many areas of our lives. We thank You for intervening in some of the difficult times of our lives, when it would have taken the improbable and impossible to see us through, yet You have worked miracles and caused them to work out in our favor– we thank You for that today!

We thank You, Father God for healing. Any ailments that affect our bodies—past or present, acute or chronic, major or minor—we thank You for healing, in the name of Jesus!

We pray for a peaceful night's sleep and for a great morning tomorrow. We pray that tomorrow will be a great day. We pray that work, church, school, etc. will be a blessing and that You will use us Lord, to love people like they need to be loved, that You will shine through us, for Your glory. In the name of Jesus we pray, amen!

_____

_____

_____

_____

_____

_____

_____

_____

_____

_____

_____

Week #3 Day 16
Title: You Are the Living Waters
Scripture: Philippians 3:13-14 (NASB)

Brethren, I do not regard myself as having laid hold of it yet; but one thing I do: forgetting what lies behind and reaching forward to what lies ahead, I press on toward the goal for the prize of the upward call of God in Christ Jesus.

Parents' Prayer:

Father God, we thank You for another day. We thank You for bringing us through this day safely and peacefully. We thank You for having your angels watch over us and not allowing any hurt, harm, or danger to come our way. And though the weapons may be formed, Father God, we praise and thank You that they will never prosper against us, in Jesus' name!

Lord God, we thank you today for forgiveness of our sins, Lord God. Just clear our souls, make our slates clean, Lord God, look at us pure as doves, Lord God. If there's anything that's not specifically planted by you in us, in our home, in our family, Lord God, uproot it in the name of Jesus and cast it down, Lord God, because we don't want anything that's not of you. Lord God, we love you today. We magnify your name. You're the Lord of lords, host of hosts, Lord God. You're the alpha, the omega. You're the beginning and the end. You're the Prince of peace. You're the Healer, the Comforter, the Counselor, Lord God.

Be with the children at school and whenever they are absent from our sight. Watch over and keep them safe, God, when we are unable to. Please watch over all of us, Lord, and bless our bodies, health, and grant us strength. We pray for living waters to flow through every aspect of our lives. Holy Spirit—You are welcome in our lives, You are welcome in our home, You are welcome in our relationships, You are welcome in our finances, You are welcome in our hearts. We pray for Your guidance and wisdom in all areas of our life—please lead us and guide us. We invite You in, Father God. The old things have passed away, and we are pressing toward the new, in Jesus' name!

We thank You and praise You for the gift of Your Holy Spirit and living waters. In Jesus' name we pray. Amen!

_____

_____

_____

_____

_____

_____

_____

_____

_____

_____

Week #3 Day 17
Title: We Welcome Your Holy Spirit into Our Home
Scripture: Psalm 91:1

Whoever dwells in the shelter of the Most High will rest in the shadow of the Almighty.

Parents' Prayer:

Father God, we thank You for another day. We worship You! We lift Your name up high above all the earth and praise You for all of the things you do. We rest in You Father God, You are our hiding place. Your Word says that He who dwells in the shelter of the Most High will rest in the shadow of the Almighty. We seek Your rest today Father God. You are our refuge and our strong tower. You are our shield, the place where we hide when we need shelter from the storms of life—and we thank You for that today.

We want to be like You, Father God; we want to be pleasing in Your sight. Help us this day, Lord. Create in us a new heart, heal our hurts. Touch our minds, grant us peace and increase our understanding, wisdom, and knowledge of Your Word that we would apply the teachings to guide ourselves through everyday life.

We pray over each and every one of our family members. You know all of the situations and circumstances. Please help each of our loved ones to know You and to trust You. Please bless our family members from the crown of their heads to the soles of their feet. If there is anything they need, we ask that You move in their lives today, Father God. We stand in the gap on behalf of our spouses, children, parents, siblings, cousins, nieces, nephews, distant relatives, friends, and anyone else You have placed in our lives. Open their eyes, clear

their minds, mend the broken, remove the doubts, and bless
them in Jesus' name.

We pray all of these things in the wonderful and precious
name of Jesus, amen!

_____

_____

_____

_____

_____

_____

_____

_____

_____

_____

_____

_____

Week #3 Day 18
Title: Renew Our Family
Scripture: Genesis 16:13a (NASB)

Then she called the name of the Lord who spoke to her,
"You are a God who sees me."

Parents' Prayer:

Father God, we thank You for this day. We thank You for this time. We thank You just for being God. We thank You for showing up today and every day! We thank You for allowing us to get home safely again once more. We know there is somebody who didn't make it home tonight; there's somebody who didn't see their family one last time. We praise and thank You on this day because that is not our story.

We ask that You forgive us of all our sins. If it's not like You, please uproot it in the name of Jesus. Create in us a new heart, transform us by renewing our minds (Romans 12:2). We put our focus on You today Father God. We trust You, we rest in You, and we accept what You allow in our lives today.

We pray specifically for the children today. We pray as they attend classes they will receive everything You would have them to receive. We pray they receive their coursework as well as any spiritual lesson/guidance You would have for them in the name of Jesus! We pray they return home with good stories and return to school in the morning well-rested.

Please bless us as we go about our day and do our jobs. Bless us to be the light for other people. Help us to be vessels for the kingdom in the marketplace. Please let us be the light and share Your word, Your love, and Your hope at our jobs. Give us the gumption and the zeal to complete our jobs with vigor and to do all things as if we were doing them for You (Colossians 3:23).

Thank You, Jesus, for all that You've done for us and all that You continue to do. Please continue to bless us and our comings and our goings, please continue to rest, rule, and abide with us now and forever more, Lord. We love You today, tomorrow, forever. In Your precious and holy name we pray, amen!

_____

_____

_____

_____

_____

_____

_____

_____

_____

_____

Week #3 Day 19
Title: Thank You Lord for the Shifting
Scripture: Luke 6:45 (NKJV)

A good man, out of the good treasure of his heart, brings forth good; and an evil man, out of the evil [a]treasure of his heart, brings forth evil. For out of the abundance of the heart his mouth speaks.

Parents' Prayer:

Dear God, we thank You for this time, we thank You for this day. Lord God, we thank You for bringing us through another day safely, heavenly Father, and we thank You for this sweet rest You're going to give us on this day. We thank You God for rejuvenating our minds, restoring our bodies, and just renewing our faith. Lord God, we pray that you continue to put Your hand of healing down. Heal the people, heal the land. Where there is any sickness, please touch and heal people in the name of Jesus.

Father, we declare and decree that these illnesses will be eradicated in Jesus' name. We pray You touch everyone in our family, everyone in our home, everyone in our immediate community, Lord God, that no one will be touched by this troubling time. That no one will be hurt, that no one will be affected by this illness.

Lord God, I thank you on today, that you are keeping us grounded, keeping us strengthened, keeping us encouraged, Lord God, in the midst of all that's going on. Lord God, the world is crazy, lonely, and cold. It's so much confusion and chaos, but Lord God, in you, we have a peace. We have a peace that surpasses all understanding. Lord God, in you, we have a counselor. In you, we have a comforter. In you, we have someone that will guide and lead us. Lord God, in your Bible, you are a pillar of cloud by day and a fire by night, to lead the way. Lord God, we thank you for your cloud of smoke. We thank you, Lord God, for your pillar of smoke and for your cloud of fire, because we know that you're leading the way. You are leading us even on today in the midst of the craziness that's going on. You're still leading us. You're still here. You're still on the cross.

You know the needs, the desires, and the wants of everyone. You know what the prayer requests are even before we utter or even think them. We put it all in Your name today, Lord God. We put them in Your precious and Holy name. In Jesus' name we pray, amen.

_____

_____

_____

_____

_____

_____

_____

_____

_____

_____

Week #3 Day 20
Title: Faith Over Fear
Scripture: 2 Timothy 1:7 (NKJV)

*For God has not given us a spirit of fear, but of power
and of love and of a sound mind.*

Parents' Prayer:

Dear God, in the name of Jesus, we thank You for this day. We thank You for this time, Lord God. We thank You for just being God. As we sit here, we just thank You God for this time to reconnect and reengage with each other. We thank You for this family time of just being together, doing things together, Lord God, and just spending time with each other.

We thank You, Lord God, that in the midst of all the turmoil, angst, and anxiety going on in the world we found time to be with each other and start praying as a family. We believe in faith that You are establishing and calling up this time right now, Lord God, that Your people might come together, that we might re-engage, reconnect, and reestablish our relationships with You and with others.

Even if the world is crazy with worry and angst, we don't operate in the spirit of fear, but Lord God, we operate in a spirit of faith. And we also walk in courage and in faith knowing that You have us, Lord God. Because of what You did on Calvary's cross, we are already healed, delivered, and set free. The blood still works, and we trust that Your blood already washes and covers all things. We trust that You're with us. We trust that You'll never leave us nor forsake us. We trust that You're holding us in Your hands.

Lord God, we thank You in advance for getting us through this season, every season, safely. We thank You in advance that no hurt, harm, or danger will come our way. We thank You in advance that no illness, affliction, or sickness will come through this threshold. We thank You in advance that no calamity will make its way in our dominion. We thank You in advance that every tactical device of the enemy will scatter on this day and it won't enter into these walls.

We frustrate any tactical device the enemy might try to throw our way, in Your name Lord God. We resist the devil and He will flee. We cast any and all evil into the pits of hell. We demand, we declare, and we decree Lord God, healing, safety, and protection for all of us, through all of our generations. We thank You in advance for touching all of our families. We thank You for just keeping us safe, in Your precious and holy name, we pray, amen.

_____

_____

_____

_____

_____

_____

_____

_____

Week #3 : Day 21
Title: We Look to the Hills
Scripture: Psalm 121:1-2 (NIV)

I lift up my eyes to the mountains— where does my help come from? My help comes from the Lord, the Maker of heaven and earth.

Parents' Prayer:

Lord God, we thank You for this day, we thank You for this time, in the name of Jesus, and we worship You here tonight Lord God. We lift our eyes and hearts to You, Lord God, with all that's going on in the world right now. We look to You, look at Your word, and it says we look to the hills on which cometh our help, Lord God (Psalm 121). Lord God, there's so many different messages and communications out there. This one says that, the other says something else, but Lord God, ultimately You are the truth, the way, and the life. All things have to come through You. All things have to bow down to You.

So Lord God, as we move towards new norms of life, as we learn to accept what you allow and don't allow, Father, as we learn to just deal with life as it comes, we do it in faith. Faith knowing that no matter what happens, You have us. Faith knowing that no matter what happens, we're to count it joy, because ultimately, it's preparing us and it's strengthening our faith. Lord God, we are to stand firm and let You move and have Your way.

Father, Your word is so rich and true! And it's sharper than any double-edged sword. So as we come here today, we thank you for the B I B L E. Thanking You for Your word, thanking You we have it as our sword, Lord God, that is our protection. That's the sword that comes… that's a part of the full armor of

You, Lord God. And with all Your armor and with Your sword, Lord God, we truly are a force to be reckoned with! And we praise and thank You for that!

Lord, we thank You. As we close out our twenty-one days of prayer… we thank You Jesus for all of the revelations You have given our family. We thank You for the answered prayers. We thank You for this time we have spent together. We ask that You continue to be with us as a family, continue to reign over us, Lord God, continue to speak through us, continue to allow us to be Your vessels, Lord God.

We ask You to continue to forgive us of our sins. We ask that You continue to just fill us with Your grace and mercy. Fill us with Your Holy Spirit. Please Lord, we ask that You continue to guide us, continue to counsel us, and continue to lead us, Lord God in the way that we should go. We always want to lean on Your understanding and not on our own, Lord God. So please, Father, just lead our thoughts, lead our understanding, lead us to health and safety. In Your precious and holy name, we pray, amen.

_____

_____

_____

_____

_____

_____

_____

SECTION #2

Kids' Prayer Journal

Week #1, Day 1
Title: Let the Journey Begin!
Scripture: Proverbs 22:6 (NIV)

Start children off on the way they should go, and even when they are old they will not turn from it.

Kids' Prayer:

God, thank You for my family, friends and teachers. Please watch over them and please keep them safe. Soften my heart and open my mind to You. Help everyone to be nice to each other and focused on You. Bless all of the adults in my life. In Jesus' name, amen.

Week #1, Day 2
Title: Open Our Eyes!
Scripture: Hosea 4:6 (KJV)

My people are destroyed for lack of knowledge.

Kids' Prayer:

God, thank You for a wonderful day. Thank You for all that You do, God. Thank You for all the wonders You have done and will continue doing. I love the things You do, God. Thank You for my family. Please let my days be good and help me always to be brave if there is something we don't like. In Jesus' name, amen.

_____

_____

_____

_____

_____

_____

_____

_____

Week #1, Day 3
Title: We Are Forgiven!
Scripture: James 5:15 (NIV)

And the prayer offered in faith will make the sick person well; the Lord will raise them up. If they have sinned, they will be forgiven.

Kids' Prayer:

God, please let everybody feel safe and okay. I pray that everyone who is sick will get healed. I pray for all the people who are lonely and don't have anyone, please put someone in their lives. I pray that everyone trusts in You. In Jesus' name, amen!

_____

_____

_____

_____

_____

_____

_____

_____

Week #1, Day 4
Title: If He Did It Before, He Can Do It Again
Scripture: Ecclesiastes 1:9 (NIV)

What has been will be again, what has been done will be done again; there is nothing new under the sun.

Kids' Prayer:

God, I pray that everyone knows You are the one true God. Please make me have a new heart, a new mind, and a new person. Please let the people who don't know You one day become Christians. Please save my unsaved loved ones. For all of my family and friends who don't know You, please let them know You and love You. Help me to show them the Word of God. Please replace/renew their hearts and fill them with love for You. In Jesus' name, I pray, amen.

_____

_____

_____

_____

_____

_____

_____

Week #1, Day 5
Title: This Is the Day That the Lord Has Made
Scripture: Psalm 118:24 (NASB)

*This is the day which the LORD has made; Let us rejoice
and be glad in it.*

Kids' Prayer:

God, I thank You for another day. I thank You for the sun, the
flowers, all the pretty nature. I pray for another beautiful day tomorrow and every day. I pray that I will not be scared or afraid.
Please help me to remember that You are always with me and
that I am never alone. Please keep me protected by Your angels.
In Jesus' name, I pray, amen.

_____

_____

_____

_____

_____

_____

_____

_____

Week #1, Day 6
Title: Give Us a Steadfast Spirit
Scripture: Psalm 51:10 (NASB)

Create in me a clean heart, O God, And renew a steadfast spirit within me.

Kids' Prayer:

God, thank You for this day. It was better than the last few of them! Thank You for all that You have done for me. Thank You for my family and all that You do for them too. Thank You for my friends, and most of all, thank You for letting Jesus come to earth. Please create in me a new heart. In Jesus' name, amen.

Week #2, Day 8
Title: We Present It All to the Father
Scripture: Philippians 4:6 (NASB)

Be anxious for nothing, but in everything by prayer and supplication with thanksgiving let your requests be made known to God.

Kids' Prayer:

Thank You God for another day. Thank You for the cross and all that You did for me and my family at the cross. Please let everyone in the world get to know and love You. I pray for the day that this world will be like heaven, where everyone will be safe and gentle. I pray for the world, for their hearts and minds. That everyone will be saved. In Jesus' name, amen.

Week #2, Day 9
Title: Bless the Children
Scripture: Psalm 8:2a (NASB)

*From the mouth of infants and nursing babes You have
established strength.*

Kids' Prayer:

God, thank You for this day. Please bless my family. I pray for
their hearts. I pray they all will have unselfish hearts. I pray
they have hearts full of God's grace, mercy, and love—like Jesus.
I want us all to see Jesus one day. Please bless us and create in
us new hearts; don't let us be angry and sad. Let us be full of joy
and peace. In Jesus' name I pray, amen.

Week #2, Day 10
Title: We Find Strength in Christ Jesus
Scripture: Psalm 46:1 (KJV)

God is our refuge and strength, A very present help in trouble.

Kids' Prayer:

God, thank You for this day. Please stop all the bad things from happening in the world. If anything bad is happening in the world, You can stop it. The whole world to belongs to You. You are our Father. You are our Savior. You're our Master, Ruler, Redeemer. Everything that You are, You are great and I love You. Please help the people of the world not be sinners, not be evil, but to be good like You and love You too. In Jesus' name, I pray, amen.

Week #2, Day 11
Title: Today We Walk in Forgiveness
Scripture: 2 Corinthians 1:4 (NASB)

...who comforts us in all our affliction so that we will be able to comfort those who are in any affliction with the comfort with which we ourselves are comforted by God.

Kids' Prayer:

God, thank You for this day. I thank You for Your loving kindness and Your patience, especially when I don't behave. I pray that everyone finds a good church home and church family to grow in the Lord together. Please let every person's heart be based on the one true God, which is You, and that they have hope and know they will receive God's riches in glory (Philippians 4:19). In Jesus' name, we pray, amen.

_____

_____

_____

_____

_____

_____

_____

Week #2, Day 12
Title: We Choose the Lord
Scripture: Joshua 25:14a (NASB)

If it is disagreeable in your sight to serve the LORD, *choose for yourselves today whom you will serve...*

Kids' Prayer:

God, thank You for this day, thank You for my family, friends, teachers. If anyone doesn't know You, I pray they will know You as their Savior. Please, God, let everybody have a warm heart, not a hardened heart like Pharaoh to Moses (*Exodus 4:21*). I pray that all are set free from sin (Romans 6:18), and that they get to know Your Son, Jesus. In Jesus' name. Amen.

_____

_____

_____

_____

_____

_____

_____

Week #2, Day 13
Title: We Choose Righteousness
Scripture: James 4:17 (NASB)

Therefore, to one who knows the right thing to do and does not do it, to him it is sin.

Kids' Prayer:

God, thank You for this day. Thank You for my family and my home. I thank You for everything You've given me. I pray for those in need, please have mercy on them this day. Please send someone to be a blessing to them. I pray for the homeless children everywhere that someone will find them and take care of them. In Jesus' name, amen.

_____

_____

_____

_____

_____

_____

_____

_____

Week #2, Day 14
Title: Keep Us in Your Perfect Peace
Scripture: 1 Peter 5:7 (NASB)

...casting all your anxiety on Him, because He cares for you.

Kids' Prayer:

God, thank You for this day. God, please save all my family members that are not saved. I pray for them today that they will not be 'half-way Christian', but that they will be all-in for You. I also pray they will read the Bible and believe Your word inside their hearts. And please replace their hard hearts, and fill them with love for you. Please let everyone in my family, neighborhood, school, and world get along. In Jesus' name, amen.

_____

_____

_____

_____

_____

_____

_____

_____

Week #3, Day 15
Title: We Claim Healing
Scripture: Psalm 34:18 (NIV)

The Lord is close to the brokenhearted and saves those who are crushed in spirit.

Kids' Prayer:

God, thank You for this day. I pray for the needy today. I pray that You will touch the heart of those with plenty, that they will not forget to share what they have with those who are in need (Hebrews 13:16). Help me share if I meet someone needy. I pray that everyone will get to know You, Jesus, and that everyone will get saved. In Jesus' name, amen!

_____

_____

_____

_____

_____

_____

_____

Week #3, Day 16
Title: You Are the Living Waters
Scripture: Philippians 3:13-14 (NASB)

Brethren, I do not regard myself as having laid hold of it yet;
but one thing I do: forgetting what lies behind and reaching
forward to what lies ahead, I press on toward the goal for the
prize of the upward call of God in Christ Jesus.

Kids' Prayer:

Dear God, we thank you for another day. We thank you for all
that you continue to do. We have good days and bad days, but
God you are always there for us. When things are scary, we
can trust you to protect us. We pray that everyone will get to
know you, not just half-way, not just a little bit—but all the way.
Please just let everybody in the world get to know you. Replace
their hearts so there will be more Christians in the world, and
that they will be okay.

Week #3, Day 17
Title: We Welcome Your Holy Spirit into Our Home
Scripture: Psalm 91:1

Whoever dwells in the shelter of the Most High will rest in the shadow of the Almighty. (NIV)

Kids' Prayer:

God, thank You for this day. I pray for everybody today, that everybody will be good. I pray for the poor, that You will supply their needs. I pray for the rich, that they will not turn their backs on the needy. I pray that everyone will think of each other, and do good for each other, like the Bible says to. I want to be saved God. If I'm not saved, please come in my heart and let me be saved and please let me have salvation. In Jesus' name I pray, amen.

_____

_____

_____

_____

_____

_____

_____

_____

Week #3, Day 18
Title: Renew Our Family
Scripture: Genesis 16:13a (NASB)

Then she called the name of the Lord who spoke to her, "You are a God who sees me."

Kids' Prayer:

God, thank You for this day. Thank You for Your love and mercy. Thank You for my home and thank You for everything that You've done. Thank You that I have family, friends, and loved ones who care for me. God, also thank You for my smart teachers. God, what would we ever do without You? No matter where we go, no matter what, You still see us and You love us. Every day You show up for me and my family. You watch over us and protect us from harm—and we thank You for that today. In Jesus' name, amen!

_____

_____

_____

_____

_____

_____

_____

Week #3, Day 19
Title: Thank You Lord for the Shifting
Scripture: Luke 6:45 (NIV)

A good man brings good things out of the good stored up in his heart, and an evil man brings evil things out of the evil stored up in his heart. For the mouth speaks what the heart is full of.

Kids' Prayer:

God, thank You for this day. Thank You for my Mommy and Daddy. If there's any bad in my mind or in my heart, please fix it. Please keep me and my family from getting sick and heal us of whatever we might have. Please touch all my family. Please let me have a good night's sleep and please let me and everyone else in my family wake up tomorrow. We pray for an amazing _____ . In Jesus' name, amen!

_____

_____

_____

_____

_____

_____

_____

Week #3, Day 20
Title: Faith Over Fear
Scripture: 2 Timothy 1:7 (NKJV)

For God has not given us a spirit of fear, but of power and of love and of a sound mind.

Kids' Prayer:

God, thank You for this day. Thank You that I can know You, and thank You for Your son. Thank You for spending my life with me and being with me even if I can't see You. Everyone needs You and You're so important to me and everybody in the world and I hope they know You. God, please let all of us have a good day and have a good night. In Jesus' name, amen.

_____

_____

_____

_____

_____

_____

_____

_____

Week #3, Day 21
Title: We Look to the Hills
Scripture: 2 Timothy 1:7 (NKJV)

For God has not given us a spirit of fear, but of power and of love and of a sound mind.

Kids' Prayer:

Thank You Lord for this day. Thank You for everything that I have, thank You for blessing others. Please bless those in need. Thank You for the B I B L E cause that's the book for me. And thank You for my family and friends and teachers. And, thank You for the three F rules... to have good friends, to have good family, and to have faith in the Almighty. The Almighty is You and I love You. Thank You for these twenty-one days of prayer with my family for the time we have been able to pray to You together. I pray we keep doing it. In Jesus' name, amen.

_____

_____

_____

_____

_____

_____

Final Thoughts

Congratulations!! You made it through twenty-one days of praying together as a family, and they say it takes twenty-one days to form a habit! Thank the Lord above—this is a good habit to have!

I pray this time has been a blessing for you all and that God has revealed some things to you all, as a family. As you enter into day twenty-two, day twenty-three and so on, please keep up the awesome work. Keep the dedicated time and space that you created as a family to complete this book! Dedicated time and space for each other and time with God is essential to keep in relationship with your heavenly Father. Because He's your Abba, He wants to be a part of your everyday life. He loves you and He loves your family.

As you continue your prayer journey, remember that the best prayers aren't the prayers that sound the most eloquent, nor are they the prayers spoken in the best or most scholarly language. Definitely not! The best prayers are those that are heartfelt, sincere, and consistent. The best prayers are those that are done in faith, obedience, and hope in the One that calls us His own. Those, dear friend, are the best prayers. Believe in God, in His word, and the knowledge He always fulfills His promises deep down inside your heart of hearts.

I have included in the appendix of this book additional prayers for daily life. There are times when we must be intentional with our prayers to get through the most difficult seasons of life. I pray these prayers offer a special blessing to you. You may pray them alone, or as a family and substitute all the singular pronouns with plural ones.

One remaining thought: in all of my prayers you will notice I end them with "In the name of Jesus, amen," or some variation of that. You may ask, "What does it mean to pray in Jesus' name?" And, "Does this guarantee my prayers will be answered?"

To answer your first question, to pray in the name of Jesus means to ask God to answer our prayers according to His character and perfect will ("Thy will be done"). However, and to address your second question, in 1 John 5:14–15, John explains to us that to pray in Jesus' name is not a magical, secret recipe for success. Not all of your prayers will be granted or answered according to your will. However, and this is the best part (even when you don't like it), ALL prayers will be answered according to God's will and in His timing, which is most definitely not synchronized with our clocks or calendars.

As believers, we have to believe and have faith that He hears all our prayers and He will answer according to His most perfect will. We must always remember that the goal of answered prayers is to bring glory to God our Heavenly Father. A sign of spiritual maturity and real growth is knowing God cannot grant a request that is not in accordance with His Character or is contrary to His perfect will. True faith is the hope that even when the answer is 'no', He will still provide for and answer according to His will, and that it will be more than we could ever ask or imagine.

Prayers for Daily Life

Salvation Prayer:

To the one that doesn't know Him yet: there's a newness of life waiting for you…no matter where you are, who you've been, or the roads you have traveled. He wants you just the way you are! And He wants all of you! Your fears, your pain, your worries… He gave His life, so that you would have life, and have it abundantly! Won't you get to know Him today? He's your Father and He loves you. Romans 10:9-10 (NIV) says:

If you declare with your mouth, "Jesus is Lord," and believe in your heart that God raised him from the dead, you will be saved. For it is with your heart that you believe and are justified, and it is with your mouth that you profess your faith and are saved.

If this is you today and you wish to follow Jesus for the first time, please pray this prayer:

Children: I want You to come into my heart as my Savior. I want to go to heaven when I die, and not hell. I want to live my life for You. In Jesus' name, I pray, amen.

Adults: Father God, I am a sinner, and there is nothing I can do to save myself. I understand that it is by Your grace alone that I am saved. And through Your mercy, I ask for Your forgiveness, that Your blood and resurrection would cover my sins and make me redeemed and perfect in Your eyes. I invite You into my heart and life as my Lord and Savior. In Jesus' name, amen.

Daily Prayer to Cover your Family:

Dear God, I thank You for another day. I thank You for allowing us to see another sunrise and another sunset. Father God, I bless and praise Your Holy name. Father God, I ask that You continue to keep my family safe and free for any hurt, harm, or danger. I ask Father God, that You would surround us with Your angels and continue to keep us safe, deliver us from evil. Lord, I ask for healing of our bodies and deliverance from strongholds.

I thank You for Your sovereignty, grace, and mercy. Father God, I thank You for being better to us than we are to ourselves. I thank You, Lord, for Your forgiveness, and thank You for always forgiving us even when we don't quite deserve to be forgiven.

Thank You for watching over my family. I ask that You continue to protect our goings out, our comings in, and all the time in between, have Your way in each and every one of our lives. I acknowledge all the individual ways I need You, Lord, that I need You to walk with me each and every day. And Lord, You said that You will give us "power to tread on serpents and scorpions and over all the power of the enemy. And nothing shall by any means hurt" us. And in Your word, You also said that "no weapon formed against us shall prosper." So Lord, I declare Your words over my life and over my family's lives today. You said the answers to Your promises are yes and amen... and I receive Your promises today.

Lord, I ask that any spirit of darkness or evil that would try to come against our family or our home, be bound in the name of Jesus. In the name of Jesus, I bind anything that is not of You. I bind any afflictions, wickedness, bad thoughts, or otherwise... I bind it all in the name of Jesus, and I loosen into the atmosphere, Father God, Your amazing grace, peace that passes all understanding, abundant love, togetherness and unity, to Your honor and glory. I pray that You continue to keep this family.

Watch over us, Father God, watch our comings and goings. I love You, Lord, I desire Your presence today and every day. In Your most precious Son's name, Jesus, I pray, amen!

COVID-19 Prayer (or any other pandemic/calamity):

I thank You for this day. I thank You for this time, Lord God, as we've been forced to stay home, and forced to social distance due to the coronavirus (or other calamities). And even though, Father, the world may be staying away and disconnecting, Lord God, I just thank You for this time and the opportunity to connect as a family. I thank You for the opportunity to spend dedicated hours together, getting to know each other better, reconnecting, laughing, learning, and just enjoying each other's company in the name of Jesus. Lord God, I thank You for this unexpected time and these most unexpected blessings of just being able to celebrate each other, see each other, and do things together, Lord God, things we normally wouldn't take the time to do.

Lord God, we're in dangerous and scary times, but I thank You for family, relationship, and perspective. That we can be together and know because of Your son, even in the worst of calamity, that You are in control. That in Your name, it will be all good in accordance with Your most perfect will. I thank You for all that You've done. I thank You for what You will continue to do, Lord God. I thank You for just being God—the same Creator of the heavens and the earth, yet Father to the orphan and Healer to the blind. I thank You for everything, Lord God. I just thank You for our family. I thank You for our home. I thank You, Lord God, even for those things that frustrate me or make me suffer, because that creates in me perseverance and character, which give me hope, and that does not disappoint or put me to shame. This is because Your love has been poured out into my heart through Your Holy Spirit (Romans 5:3-5).

Lord God, I pray for the people who are sick and afflicted with this illness and disease (or other illnesses). Lord God, I pray for the families of those who have lost loved ones due to the virus (or other illnesses). I pray for those who are struggling right now. I pray for those who have preexisting health conditions and are high risk and are unable to do anything they would want or need to do, Lord God. I cover all of those individuals in prayer, in Your name.

It's important that each and everyone know that they are not alone, Lord God, and know they have other people who care and are praying for them. Heavenly Father, if anybody is dealing with a spirit of rejection, a spirit of loneliness tonight, or even a spirit of adversity and affliction Lord, let them rebuke it in Your name! I pray with them, Lord. I stand in the gap with them. I declare and decree that they will be whole, that they will have the love and comfort of the Holy Spirit! That Your Spirit will totally and completely consume them to the point that they don't have those thoughts or feelings anymore.

I love You, Lord God. I thank You in advance for all that You've done and all that You continue to do for me and my family. And now in Your precious and Holy name, I pray. Amen.

Physical Healing Prayer:

Father God, I specifically pray for my sick and/or afflicted love ones on this day. Father God, I pray that You would touch the hands of the doctors. Send down Your Holy spirit to fill each and every doctor, nurse, technician and all of the other medical staff members with wisdom and knowledge only You can provide. Fill the entire medical facility with the Holy Spirit, Father God, that each and every thought, and decision, and movement of a medical instrument, Father God, is done in according to Your perfect will. I ask, Lord, tonight, that if the doctors and nurses do not know You and aren't saved, that they turn to You, Lord, that they open their hearts and invite You in, Father God. That they would believe in Your son's death and resurrection for the covering of their sins. That they operate and care for my loved ones, Father God, under Your anointing.

Father God, I ask that You heal the bodies of my loved ones. I know, believe, and stand in authority that, by Your stripes, he/she is already healed, Father God. You've already defeated this illness/sickness/infirmity at the cross. I stand, Almighty God, asking that You send Your angels down to protect him or her. Send a hedge of protection around him or her, Lord, as they have the appointment/procedure. I pray they will not only be okay, but that they'll have peace of mind, and a quick, speedy recovery and healing. In Jesus' name I pray, amen!

Prayer to Heal Family Divisions:

Lord God, I ask that You be with all of us, Lord God, that You would be with the family. If there's any divisions, or agendas, or things trying to keep any of us apart or away, Lord God, straighten out what's crooked, make right anything that's wrong. Father, there's a path that is good—a way of decency and order. That applies to the family structure as well, Lord God. I just pray if there's anything among the family that's done in the darkness, that it comes to Your light, Lord God. If the family is blinded by perceptions that are wrong, Father, I pray that You would illuminate with the truth. I pray that our intentions be pure, that all can see and understand how everyone else feels and how things are perceived, Lord God. May we treat each other with love, patience, grace and mercy. Fruits of Your most holy and precious Spirit.

Sometimes, Lord God, family members can be offensive without meaning to offend. So Father, I'm praying for a lack of offenses. I'm praying, Lord God, for togetherness and unity in the family, because that's what we need. In the name of Jesus, Lord God, I pray, worship You, honor You. I magnify Your Holy name, Lord God. I am praying, resting in, and asking for a mighty moving of the Holy Spirit to save my loved ones that are not saved, to bring them closer to You, Lord God. In the name of Jesus, I pray, amen.

Prayer for Parental Discipline:

Dear Lord, I pray specifically for our little one(s). Touch his/her soul. Touch his/her heart, touch his/her mind. He/She's so smart and mature and perceives so much, Lord God. But he/she's a little sad today. He/She understands that he/she did wrong and there are consequences for it, that he/she may be punished for it. But he/she's sad nonetheless. So, Lord God, just touch his/her heart. Make sure he/she knows that his/her parent(s) love him/her. But at the same time, in order for us to be good parents, we have to discipline the things that are done wrong. But Lord God, may he/she know that no matter what, as parents, he/she will always be first in our lives, Lord God, after You.

Please touch his/her mind, that he/she knows for sure, Lord God that his/her parents have his/her back and that we love him/her. And that discipline is only for a moment. That he/she is going to be just fine. We know no one likes to be reproved. No one likes to be rebuked. No one likes to be disciplined, but it's necessary for all of us. And so, Lord God, we ask that You touch his/her heart. Send Your angels and Your cherubim down, Father. Surround him/her. I dedicate him/her and lift him/her up to You, Lord God, and ask that he/she understands exactly what we expect of him/her, that he/she understands exactly what You expect of him/her, Lord God.

He/She is a child of God. And that's a lot to be responsible for. So Lord God, I just ask that You continue to bless us today. Forgive us of our sins, Lord God. Forgive him/her of the things that he/she did. Forgive me of the things that I have done. Forgive all of us, Lord God. We repent. We turn over our wicked ways in submission to You. We reach up for You, Almighty Father, Creator of Heaven and earth, and all that dwells in it. In Jesus's name we pray, amen!

About the Author

A servant of God, Minister Nikkia 'Kia' Durham strives for excellence in ministry through the Word of God, the work of God, and the will of God. She sincerely loves God and God's people; therefore, she professes boldly the words of Luke 4:18, "The Spirit of the Lord is on me, because He has anointed me to proclaim good news to the poor. He has sent me to proclaim freedom for the prisoners and recovery of sight for the blind, to set the oppressed free..."

Minister Kia is a military wife, mother, sister, daughter, friend, intercessor, YouTuber, blogger, and student of the Gospel. In 2015, Minister Kia accepted her calling from the Lord to pursue ministry for the kingdom of God. Although Minister Kia had been serving in ministry for many years, to include teaching Bible Study classes to French children while studying abroad in Paris, it was at this time that she received a word from God to be an example and advocate women, children, and families—everywhere.

In 2017, Minister Kia pursued her license in ministry by attending a yearlong minister's development institute. This program can be viewed as pre-seminary in that it challenges its students to think higher in how things relate to sharing the Gospel of Jesus. Her mission is to uplift and empower all of God's people, emphasizing working mothers who are juggling careers, children, marriages, wellness, etc. Many have said that women can't have it all, but by the grace of God and the power of the Holy Spirit, Minister Kia has found that all things are possible with God. This message is one that Minister Kia looks to share around the world.

In 2020, Minister Kia started the "Faith Talks with Kia" YouTube Channel, where she addresses real-life issues from a Biblical perspective. Minister Kia is also a standing host on the Friendz and the Fam Podcast, where the hosts tackle very real issues affecting the African American community every day. Minister Kia is also a huge advocate for mental health awareness. She is a Mental Health First Aid Responder and is currently pursuing her National Certification in Christian Counseling.

In addition to ministry, Minister Kia is a full-time working mother. She is married to her high school sweetheart of over twenty years, Anthony Durham. They have two beautiful children, Nia and Anthony, Jr. They currently attend Highview Christian Fellowship under the leadership of Bishop Phillip O. Thomas in Fairfax, Virginia.

Minister Kia is a Lead Associate with the Booz Allen Hamilton (Booz Allen) consulting firm. Before joining Booz Allen, Minister Kia worked as a Program Manager for the Federal Government in Washington, DC for over fourteen years.

Minister Kia's hobbies and interests include learning to play the piano, bike-riding, walks by the lake, reading, spending time with loved ones, and studying the Word of God. Minister Kia and her family are actively pursuing Black Belts in American Freestyle Karate.

Minister Kia graduated from the Fox School of Business and Management at Temple University in Philadelphia, PA, with an International MBA (IMBA). The focus of her IMBA is strategy management. She also has a Bachelor of Science degree in Computer Science and Math theory from Stockton College in Pomona, New Jersey.

Connect and Share

If you enjoyed this book, please consider purchasing copies for your family, friends, and neighbors. Be sure to leave a review on Amazon.com, and connect with the author online. Visit:

MinisterKia.com

Instagram.com/ministerkia

Facebook.com/ministerkia

Youtube.com: Faith Talks with Kia